Provided
by

Measure B

which was approved by
the voters in
November, 1998

LATINOS IN THE LIMELIGHT

Christina Aguilera   John Leguizamo

Antonio Banderas   Jennifer Lopez

Jeff Bezos   Ricky Martin

Oscar De La Hoya   Pedro Martínez

Cameron Diaz   Freddie Prinze Jr.

Scott Gomez   Selena

Salma Hayek   Carlos Santana

Enrique Iglesias   Sammy Sosa

CHELSEA HOUSE PUBLISHERS

LATINOS
IN THE
LIMELIGHT

Salma Hayek

Kieran Scott

CHELSEA HOUSE PUBLISHERS
Philadelphia

Frontis: Salma Hayek uses her success to work on projects close to her heart, and has convinced critics and fans alike that good acting has a universal appeal.

CHELSEA HOUSE PUBLISHERS

Editor in Chief: Sally Cheney
Director of Production: Kim Shinners
Production Manager: Pamela Loos
Art Director: Sara Davis
Editor: Bill Conn
Production Editor: Diann Grasse

Layout by
21st Century Publishing and Communications, Inc.
http://www.21cpc.com

The Chelsea House World Wide Web address is
http://www.chelseahouse.com

First Printing

1 3 5 7 9 8 6 4 2

Library of Congress Cataloging-in-Publication Data

Scott, Kieran, 1974–
        Salma Hayek / Kieran Scott.
            p. cm. — (Latinos in the limelight)
        Includes bibliographical references.
        Summary: Profiles the Mexican-born actress whose pet project, a biographical film based on the life of Mexican artist Frida Kahlo, is now in production due in large part to Salma's initiative.
        ISBN 0-7910-6476-X (alk. paper)
        1. Hayek, Salma, 1968-   —Juvenile literature. 2. Actors—Mexico—Biography—Juvenile literature. [1. Hayek, Selma, 1968–
2. Actors and actresses. 3. Women—Biography.] I. Title. II. Series.

PN2318.H39 S38 2001
791.43'028'092—dc21
    [B]   2001042477

CONTENTS

THE FIGHT FOR FRIDA

Salma Hayek does not take no for an answer. At five-foot-two inches tall and about 106 pounds, she may look like someone who'd be easy to push around, but that's anything but true. When Salma was a 12-year-old girl growing up in Mexico and wanted to go to Catholic school in the United States, she worked on her parents until they let her go. When she wanted to become an actress against all her friends' and family members' better judgment, she went out and made a name for herself on the small screen in her home country. When everyone told her a Mexican TV actress would have no shot at making it in Hollywood, Salma proved them wrong in a major way.

So when it seemed like Salma's pet project—a biographical film of legendary Mexican artist Frida Kahlo—would never get made, Salma did everything in her power to make sure her dream of bringing this heroine's life to the screen would come true.

Salma was first exposed to Kahlo's paintings when she was about 14 years old. At the time, she didn't really like Kahlo's work. "I found it ugly and grotesque," Salma

---

Salma's natural beauty and sense of style has put her on the covers of film and fashion magazines around the world. However, she does take time out of her Hollywood schedule to help the less fortunate. Here, she donates her time to a relief effort in Kosovo.

has said. "But something intrigued me, and the more I learned, the more I started to appreciate her work." It's not surprising that a young girl would find Kahlo's paintings disturbing. The painter, who is known for her self-portraits, did not necessarily paint herself in the most beautiful light. The colors are dark and the textures are rough, so a child might not be drawn to the images. It takes a closer look to see that Kahlo was also painting self-portraits of a strong, defiant woman who beat the odds—a woman who became one of the most revered artists of her time. In fact, in the 1990s, one of Kahlo's paintings, "Self-Portrait with Monkey and Parrot," broke records, earning the highest price ever paid for a Latin American painting— $3.2 million.

The more Salma learned about Frida Kahlo, the more fascinated she was with the artist's life story. The woman was a rule-breaker, a true romantic, and a strong, original spirit. Born in 1907, Kahlo had a bout with polio as a young girl and then was hit by a streetcar at the age of 18. The accident shattered her pelvis, left her nearly paralyzed, and made it impossible for her to ever have children. But Kahlo didn't let the tragedy stop her. In fact, she used her pain to enrich her work, and at the age of 20, she showed some of her paintings to the world-famous Mexican artist Diego Rivera. Rivera fell in love with Kahlo and left his wife to marry her. But Kahlo's troubles didn't end when her romance began. In fact, her life only got more dramatic. Even though the couple traveled all over the world, fascinating people with their glamorous, irreverent life style, Kahlo's life continued to

After a decade of struggles, Salma's biographical film about the life of Mexican artist Frida Kahlo, shown here, is finally set for release on *Showtime*. Bringing strong Latina women into the spotlight has always been a goal for Salma.

be tumultuous. She and Rivera both had affairs, and when Rivera actually courted her sister, Kahlo divorced him . . . only to remarry him a year later. When Kahlo died at the young age of 47, she'd lived more life than most people do in twice that time.

Kahlo's life story contains more than enough drama to make a Hollywood film, but bringing the story to the silver screen has been a struggle that has taken well over 10 years.

The first person to realize the potential of Kahlo's story was Nancy Hardin, an independent film producer. In 1988 she read a biography of Frida Kahlo written by an author named Hayden Herrera. At that point, Hardin was just getting into the film producing game, and Kahlo was practically unknown in the United States—but Hardin was so blown away by Kahlo's story, she took her idea for a biographical movie of the artist to every single production company in Hollywood. Unfortunately, every single production company rejected it. "Nobody at the studios had heard of Frida at the time," Hardin recalls. "And there was no interest in Latin America."

Luckily, that fact has changed. With the Latin music boom, actors and actresses like Salma, Jennifer Lopez, and Antonio Banderas making headlines, and the growing population of Latin citizens in the United States, Hollywood is finally waking up to the importance of Latin American culture. The moviemaking industry is also beginning to recognize the fact that films appealing to the Latin American population can bring in big box-office money.

When Hardin was trying to sell her movie, there were no well-known Latin American actresses to take the part, but in the mid-'90s, Salma emerged as the perfect candidate. She had turned heads in movies like *Desperado* and *From Dusk Til Dawn*, but she wasn't just another pretty face. Directors and producers had come to respect her acting, and Salma was making a name for herself as a person who was willing to take risks. Salma expressed her interest in playing Frida, and just like that, Trimark Pictures agreed to develop the project with her and Hardin. The production company was dying to work with this hot young star.

Finally, it seemed as if the movie would be made. But it wasn't to be. The studio executive who had been working with Salma and Hardin left Trimark, and no one else at the company was willing to continue with the project. Things were looking grim, so Salma took matters into her own hands.

Salma had worked on a lot of films with Miramax—the company known for helping Matt Damon, Ben Affleck, and Gwyneth Paltrow jumpstart their careers. Knowing that Miramax head Harvey Weinstein was always looking for interesting projects in which he could feature his favorite young actors, Salma secretly took the Frida Kahlo project to him. Miramax bought the rights, investing a ton of money, and now, thanks to Salma's determination, the Frida Kahlo story is finally in production. The cast is filling up with superstars fast, and the list also includes many of Salma's close friends. Her boyfriend, Edward Norton Jr., who was nominated for an Oscar for *Primal Fear*, is taking a small role, and Ashley Judd and Antonio Banderas have also signed on to play parts in the film.

Salma should have been able to breathe a huge sigh of relief. The film that had become "a project of obsession" was finally coming together. Unfortunately, Miramax was having trouble finding the right director for the film. After talking with many candidates, losing out on a few, and rejecting a few, a director was finally attached to the project in September 2000. Julie Taymor, the Tony-winning director

Bringing strong Latina women into the limelight has always been Salma's goal. After lobbying hard to have the Frida Kahlo story told, she achieved victory when Miramax agreed to pursue the project.

of the Broadway musical *The Lion King*, signed on to direct the film. Salma, who had always said she would be ready to go to work the moment a director was found, was ecstatic.

She had seen many of her dreams come true over the years, but this was a victory like no other. Bringing strong Latina women into the spotlight has always been a driving goal for Salma. Now, not only would she be starring as one of her country's enduring heroines, but her production company, Ventanarosa, would co-produce the film. Salma had come a long way from her early days in Hollywood when she barely spoke a word of English and didn't know how to navigate her way around town.

She had grown to a position of power in one of the most cutthroat cities in the world. But to hear her tell the story, she never had any doubt about how her life would play out.

2

GROWING UP
SALMA STYLE

Salma Hayek Jimenez was born on September 2, 1968 in Coatzacoalcos, Veracruz, Mexico. Coatzacoalcos is a beautiful port town on the gulf coast of Mexico—a place where the extremely wealthy live alongside the extremely poor. Salma was on the luckier side of the coin, growing up in a privileged household with a family full of love. Her father, Sami Hayek Dominguez, who is of Lebanese descent, was a top executive with the state-owned oil company; he brought home a sizable salary. Diana Hayek, Salma's mother, came from a Spanish background; she is a former opera singer and teacher, who now scouts young talent and helps secure scholarships for children who wish to study singing.

Salma also has a younger brother, Sami, her constant companion growing up who was always protective of her. She was with Sami when she went to a shabby movie theater to catch a showing of *Willy Wonka and the Chocolate Factory* and decided to become an actress. (After seeing the film she couldn't understand why anyone would want to do anything other than act.) Years later, after

---

Veracruz is a beautiful port town on Mexico's gulf coast where the wealthy and the poor live side-by-side. It's also the place where Salma was born and grew up with her parents and brother. Here, after seeing her first movie, she decided to become an actress.

Salma became famous, Sami watched over her even more closely than he did when they were young. "He gets so protective when fans follow me," Salma told *Scene* magazine. "He would be the one who punched someone while my boyfriend would hear the other side of the story first." Sami is still there whenever Salma needs him. He even renovated her house in Los Angeles, turning a basic 1950s design into an exotic Mexican-style abode so Salma would feel at home.

Salma's grandmother was also a big part of her life as a child. Salma may even have Grandma to thank for some of her incredible beauty. When Salma was little, her grandmother often shaved Salma's head and clipped her eyebrows, believing this would make her hair grow in thicker and shinier. It seems her tactics may have worked.

By all accounts, Salma was an adventurous, headstrong, mischievous little girl. She has no problem telling reporters that she was spoiled and led a charmed life as a child. "I thought I was a princess," Salma told *Scene.* "I lived in a castle and my father was a king. I wore tiaras. I was born diva-ish." True to young diva form, Salma developed a love of clothes and high fashion when she was little. "When other kids were getting excited about toys, I would get excited about clothes," Salma told *Elle* magazine. She recounted a story about a special jacket she received from her parents when she was as young as five. Her mother and father brought the trench coat home from a trip, and Salma loved it so much, she wanted to wear it to school. Unfortunately, it was much too hot in Mexico to wear such a heavy coat, but

Independent film director Robert Rodriguez, seen here, gave Salma her first big break when he cast her in *Desperado*.

Salma wouldn't take no for an answer. She and her mother got into huge fights about it.

Since she was little, Salma's strict sense of style has only blossomed. She is still obsessive about clothing today, always making sure she wears something original and eye-catching to every premiere, party, and charity event. She loves to break the stereotypes that Mexicans are tacky dressers and that serious actresses aren't into fashion. Open any *In Style* or *People* magazine, and you'll undoubtedly find Salma breaking those stereotypes.

But clothes weren't her only extravagant hobby when she was a kid. Salma also loved to swim and water ski in the Gulf of Mexico. She adored animals as well, but she didn't have your run-of-the-mill pets. Not only did Salma keep her own horses (she loves to ride), but she also had her own private zoo that housed a series of pet tigers!

A lot of parents don't even like to keep a tabby cat in the house, but Salma's indulgent parents allowed her favorite tiger Rambo to roam the halls and keep Salma company in her bedroom. Unfortunately, Rambo died in an accident that was so traumatic for Salma, she doesn't even like to talk about it today.

The Hayek family traveled a lot when Salma was a child. Every summer they would spend the holidays in the Greek Islands, and in the winter they would head to Colorado for some serious skiing.

This early exposure to foreign lands may have contributed to Salma's decision, at a very young age, to ditch her school in Mexico and head for the States. When she was just 12 years old, Salma begged her parents to send her to a Catholic school in Louisiana, and she didn't stop until she got her way. A lot of other Mexican children were boarding at the school, and Salma made friends easily, conversing primarily in Spanish—a move she would later regret. Although today Salma says she is not a good Catholic, back then she was a religious student and got excellent grades. But she still managed to get kicked out of school two years after she enrolled. Why? She was also a serious practical jokester.

Salma would constantly play pranks on other students and on the nuns who taught at her school, and she was always reprimanded. But one infamous prank was the straw that broke the camel's back. Salma snuck into the dormitory where her teachers lived and set all the alarm clocks back three hours. The students got to snag a little extra sleep, but when Salma was found out, she was sent packing back to Mexico.

Salma completed her education back home, and graduated high school early, at the age of 16. She wanted to go right to college, but her mother thought she was a little too young to be exposed to university life—and college-aged boys. Instead, Salma went off to Houston, Texas, to live with a favorite aunt for four months, until she turned 17. Salma says she went through a bit of a rebellious period at this age—dressing like a punk and still refusing to learn English. But the phase ended quickly, and soon Salma was enrolled in the Universidad Iberoamericana in Mexico City where she majored in international relations studies and drama.

Her study and love of drama was what changed her life.

When Salma was 18 years old, she stunned her parents and family with her decision to drop out of college and pursue an acting career full time. "One day I took my dad to lunch. I asked him if he believed in destiny and he said, 'Yes.' And I said, 'Well, I believe it's my destiny to become an actress,'" Salma said in a Mr. Showbiz interview. Whether or not her father believed in destiny, he didn't take well

Although the film *Wild Wild West* was less than successful than her other ventures, Salma's performance earned her a Blockbuster Award for Favorite Supporting Actress in 2000.

to the idea that Salma was meant to be on stage or in front of the cameras. He was worried about his little girl's future stability. And he wasn't the only one with doubts.

"I'd always wanted to be an actress," Salma told *Scene* magazine. "When I left school to pursue it, my parents didn't take it lightly. My friends thought it was the tackiest thing they'd ever heard." Eventually, her friends would come around. And after some major discussions, Salma finally convinced her parents she was serious about this major life decision.

They were even more convinced when Salma quickly started to succeed.

MEXICO'S
MEGA-STAR

After Salma had won her family over to her decision, she went about trying to break into the acting business in a very practical manner. The girl who had always been so brazen and had spent a lifetime grabbing whatever she wanted, realized she had some work to do if she really wanted to act. "I never committed to anything until acting," Salma says. Taking that commitment seriously, Salma didn't run out and try to snag an agent and become an overnight sensation. She started in local theater where she could be on stage and learn more about the craft that would eventually become her profession.

Salma's first auditions were for small roles in neighborhood theaters. Like any other actress just starting out, she won some and lost some. Her first break came when she landed the lead female role of Jasmine in the play *Aladdin and His Marvelous Lamp*. It was a children's play, and Salma was so convincing and beautiful in the role of the heroine, children used to call out to her and try to climb up onto the stage to be close to her. Already, Salma's star power was undeniable.

After working in theater for several months, Salma

After beginning her career acting in Mexican commercials and soap operas, Salma achieved mega-stardom through her work in Hollywood films like *Desperado* and *From Dusk Till Dawn*.

landed a few commercials. But her stage work was what led her to a level of stardom she never could have imagined.

One day in 1988, after taking her bows on stage, Salma was approached by a prime-time soap opera producer. The prime-time soap is one of the most popular forms of television programming in Mexico, so when the producer said he wanted to work with Salma, she was ecstatic. This was her big chance to make it as an actress and prove to everyone that she'd made the right decision. Salma was first cast in a small role in the soap opera *Un Nuevo Amanecer* (*A New Dawn*). She had been there for less than a year when she won the role that would change her life.

Teresa was a new soap opera about a poor 18-year-old girl who was completely unsatisfied with her position in life. She was a sexy, outrageous social climber who would do everything in her power to achieve her one goal—absolute wealth. The show was melodramatic, weepy, silly, fun, and completely out-there. And it was a runaway hit—one of the most popular shows on Mexican television.

Salma was its star.

Through her role as Teresa, Salma Hayek became the single most recognizable actress in all of Mexico. She was followed around on the streets by her fans, and constantly had to disguise herself just so she could leave her home. "The country worships its stars. And it enslaves them mercilessly," Salma said to *Vivamagazine*. "When you are popular in Mexico, you don't have a single moment to yourself anymore." Having so many fans was also a bit scary. "American audiences are not as passionate, you know. They just stare at you . . . in a state of panic," Salma said in another Mr. Showbiz interview. "In Mexico, when you know that they are coming over, you're the one that panics." This was both a happy and stressful time for Salma. While she was making her living doing what she loved the most, she was also unable to live a normal life. During her stint as Teresa, she returned to the stage to act in a play called *Bedroom Farce*, and her fans rushed the stage. Salma's life was no longer her own.

In 1989, Salma won two TV Novela Awards (the Mexican equivalent of an Emmy). One was for Best Newcomer in *Un Nuevo Amanecer*, and the other was for Best Actress in *Teresa*. Salma stuck with the show until 1991, when she made another radical decision. Tired of what she considered to be the poor quality of government-financed television in Mexico, Salma decided to leave the show and her country and head for Los Angeles. She wanted to see if she could make it outside the glow of stardom she'd developed in Mexico.

"I was so successful in my early years— I knew the camera liked me," Salma told *Vivamagazine*. "I was famous, but how good was I, really? That's why I went to Hollywood."

Her decision shocked her fans and broke hearts across her country. A rumor was even started that Salma had had an affair with Mexico's president and that Salma had to leave to avoid the anger of the president's wife. It wasn't true, though. Salma left it all behind—the fame, the riches, her home and family—because she wanted to prove she was truly a good actress. It was a crazy, brave move. And for a while, it seemed Salma might have made a huge mistake.

When Salma first arrived in Los Angeles in 1991, two obstacles obviously stood in the way of her success. Unfortunately, they were big obstacles.

First, she could not drive. In a city like New York, which has buses and subways and taxis that can take you anywhere, this wouldn't have been such a problem. But L.A. is a city of freeways, expressways, and highways. It's practically impossible to get around without a car. So Salma had to learn to drive.

First, she tried driving stick shift, which she gave up after two days; learning a manual while trying to make her way around Los Angeles was pointless. Salma got herself an automatic car and a cell phone, just in case she needed help or directions—but her troubles were not over. "My bill on that phone was so outrageous!" Salma told *Los Angeles Magazine*. "I was always so lost . . . I would get on the phone and drive my friends crazy. I would stay on the line the whole time because I'd get so lost and always at the wrong places. I'd be on the phone, crying for hours in East L.A., crying for hours in South-Central." One time Salma even found herself in San Francisco, hundreds of miles north of Los Angeles, when all she was trying to do was get to Burbank.

Salma's other obstacle—the bigger and more crucial one—was her inability to speak English. This was when she really started to regret not learning English in school when she'd had the chance. Casting directors weren't hiring actresses that couldn't speak the language, so Salma ended up taking 18 months off from acting while she took rigorous English classes and studied acting under a famous dramatist named Stella Adler. This

Launched into the glamorous world of Hollywood, Salma found herself attending many prestigious parties and receptions. Here she is at a party to honor singing legend Frank Sinatra.

was a tough time for Salma, and she says she went through a period of confusion and insecurity. Here she was in a strange country where she barely spoke the language, without her family, without a boyfriend, with no job and constantly getting lost. That would cause anyone to be insecure.

Finally, after months of working on her skills and her accent, Salma felt she was ready to start auditioning. Her first break in the film business doesn't sound like a huge success, but it meant a lot to her career. In 1993 Salma auditioned for a film called *Mi Vida Loca (My Crazy Life)*. She was given callback after callback, and in the end, had auditioned for the lead role for four months straight. Unfortunately, Salma lost the part, but the director of the film, Allison Anders, was impressed by Salma's determination. To reward her for never giving up, Anders gave Salma a few small roles so that Salma could get her Screen Actors Guild card. (Actors need the card to be in the actors' union. Without it, they are barred from working on most projects.)

After getting her SAG card, Salma landed a series of minor roles on the small screen. Her first television appearance in the United States was as the wife of a gang member on a syndicated crime show called *Street Justice*. It wasn't exactly *Teresa*, but it was something. She followed it up with guest spots on not-so-popular sitcoms like *The Sinbad Show* and *Nurses*, and another guest spot on the more respected HBO comedy, *Dream On*. They were small, mostly stereotypical roles, but while this was frustrating for Salma, she didn't let it get her down. "People asked me if I felt humiliated testing for small roles after being so famous in my home country, but I said no," Salma told *Scene*.

The size of the roles wasn't what irritated Salma. She knew she had to pay her dues. What irritated her was the stereotyping. Most of her parts were all about her sex appeal. Salma felt that her acting ability didn't really matter to the people who had cast her; she was just the exotic, Mexican babe in the tight dress. This made her angry, and she wasn't going to take it anymore. Her anger turned out to be a good thing.

In 1994, Salma appeared in the Spanish-language talk show, *The Paul Rodriguez Show*, on the Spanish-language network, Univision. She and Rodriguez, the show's host, got to talking about the stereotyping of Hispanic actors and actresses, and Salma became impassioned, speaking about an issue in which she was so deeply involved. Little did she know that this one conversation would help her land her first starring role in a major motion picture.

Mexican-American independent film director Robert Rodriguez (no relation to the talk-show host) happened to be watching the show in which Salma appeared. He and his wife, Elizabeth Avellan, a producer, were both mesmerized by the fiery, explosive actress who lit up their TV screen. At the time, Rodriguez was working on casting a new film called *Desperado*, a follow-up to his hit film *El Mariachi*. The moment Rodriguez saw Salma, he knew he wanted her to play the role of Carolina, the heroine of the story. "She was so [gutsy] on TV, saying how the state of the entertainment industry was toward Latinas," Rodriguez said. "I wanted to put Salma on screen just the way she was." The next day he set about tracking Salma down. When he finally contacted her, he offered her the role and a shocked yet pleased Salma accepted. It was as simple as that, right? Not quite.

Rodriguez's financial backers didn't agree with his choice. They wanted a tall blonde to play the role of Carolina—an idea Rodriguez thought was ridiculous. But he understood that his partners needed some convincing.

Luckily, he had already been hired to direct an episode of the Showtime series, *Rebel Highway.* Rodriguez cast Salma in his episode, titled "Roadracers," so that Salma could show off her acting abilities. She did, and she won over Rodriguez's partners. Salma Hayek was about to make a big splash on the big screen.

Desperado was a huge action hit in the summer of 1995, thrusting its star, Antonio Banderas, into Hollywood's limelight. Salma couldn't have been more excited about her big screen debut. Her time had finally come. Or had it?

After the movie wrapped, Salma thought, "I've made it! This is it!" But nothing happened. The offers did not role in. The phone did not start ringing. Salma was not the next big thing of 1995. Perhaps Hollywood wasn't yet ready to accept a Mexican leading lady with exotic looks and a thick accent. If that was the case, then maybe it was time to go home and show her country how much she appreciated what they had done for her. And that's exactly what Salma did. In 1995, she starred in another film, this one made in Mexico. It was called *El Callejon de los milagros.* (*Miracle Alley*), and it was a major critical success. It's the story of a neighborhood in Mexico City and the interwoven lives of the people that live there. Salma was nominated for a Silver Ariel award—the Mexican equivalent of the Oscar— for her role as Alma, a local sweetheart who becomes a prostitute when her boyfriend runs off to the United States.

The film was an international success, winning over 50 awards all over the world. It was also Mexico's entry for Best Foreign Film

Director Robert Rodriguez was impressed by Salma's talent and insisted she co-star with Antonio Banderas in *Desperado* — a huge action hit released in the summer of 1995.

at the Academy Awards. It's recognized as one of the best films ever made in Mexico. Salma had proven to herself she was still a great actress and capable of great things. It was time to get back to the States and give her career there another shot.

4

BREAKING DOWN WALLS

Feeling accomplished and assured of her talents, Salma returned to Los Angeles and started auditioning again. It still wasn't easy. Producers, directors, and casting directors continued to pigeonhole Salma as the sexy Mexican seductress.

Robert Rodriguez cast her in a very small role in his installment of the film *Four Rooms*. The movie included four vignettes, each directed by a different director. Salma was happy to take the tiny part in her friend's film. She followed this brief appearance up with another small role in a little-seen film called *Fair Game*.

This action/drama movie was supposed to turn super model Cindy Crawford into an acting star. It didn't exactly work. There was no real audience for *Fair Game*, and very few people have ever seen Salma's performance as Rita, the former lover of Crawford's costar, William Baldwin.

Around the same time, Robert Rodriguez asked Salma to appear in his next film—one he was working on with writer/director Quentin Tarantino, who had just hit it big with *Pulp Fiction*. Rodriguez told Salma she was his good luck charm and that she had to take the part. But one look

Combining action, horror, and comedy, the vampire film *From Dusk Till Dawn* scored Salma another hit a year after *Desperado*. She is seen here with her son, Rocket, on opening night.

at the script nearly scared Salma off. Not only did the part of Satanico—a female vampire—require her to dance, which she'd never done on screen before, but she had to dance with a snake! A six-foot-long python, to be exact. Salma had an incredible fear of snakes, so the idea of acting in this scene terrified her. Still, she agreed to take the part; Salma is always up for a challenge, so she had to find a way to get through it.

Salma tried everything, from hanging out at a pet store to be close to snakes, to meditation, to reading about snakes and their significance to certain cultures, but nothing worked. Finally, a film producer who was a longtime friend of Salma's, performed a ritual on her that was supposed to rid her of her fear. Salma didn't really believe it had worked until the time came to shoot the scene: she was fine. Her dance scene is one of the most memorable of the film.

But the snake wasn't the only difficult thing to handle on the set of *From Dusk Til Dawn.* The movie is about two men, played by George Clooney and Quentin Tarantino, who rob a bank in Texas and then flee to Mexico. When they get there they stop at a bar, and quickly discover it's full of vampires. Salma was one of those demons, and transforming her beautiful features into the hideous vampire's face took a lot of time and discomfort. Salma would have to sit in the makeup trailer for hours while the makeup artists used complicated chemicals and prosthetics to change her face. Her reward? People on the set wouldn't go near her once she was made up.

"I was the same girl underneath the mask, but everyone avoided me," Salma told Mr.

Showbiz. "They didn't even want to look at me. I really learned what it's like for people who have deformities. We don't want to see through to the person. It's really terrible. I was really depressed." Still, Salma enjoyed working on *From Dusk Til Dawn*, if only because she was surrounded by men who loved to take risks. "Robert and Quentin never think, 'Is this going to work, is this not going to work? Is someone going to like it, or are they not going to like it?' They have something to say and they just say it. They have no fear," Salma said. For someone known to take a few risks herself, Salma must have felt right at home on the set.

From Dusk Til Dawn earned itself a cult following and mixed reviews, but Salma took away a few good things from the experience. She'd gotten over her fear of snakes, she'd made friendships with Clooney and Tarantino she still values today, and she'd had the chance to work with Robert Rodriguez once again.

Next, Salma took another minor role in a small film called *Fled*. Starring Laurence Fishburne and Stephen Baldwin, the movie is a comedy about two escaped convicts who are chained together and are fleeing from the Cuban mafia. Salma played Fishburne's love interest who helps the two criminals get away. Like *Fair Game*, it was neither a critical nor financial success. But for the first time, Salma was able to display her considerable comedic talents, impressing her costars and even getting the chance to write a few jokes for herself.

The same year, Salma was approached by producers who were putting together a biographical movie of Latina pop star Selena. The producers asked Salma if she'd be interested in reading for the role—she was, in fact, their first choice for the part—but Salma turned them down. "Selena has a tremendous following, and I think the movie is going to be a hit. But she just died; it's been barely two years," Salma said at the time. "The people involved in the project are great people; I'm not questioning their intentions . . .but you have to make a choice about what things you do in life."

Instead of taking the big money and starring in *Selena*, Salma took the role in *Fled* and followed it up with a part in a very small film called *Breaking Up*. This movie starred Russell Crowe, who was then still unknown; Salma says she took the part of Monica because it was brilliantly written. Even though the movie was little seen, Salma was very proud of it. Of her work on these two films, she said, "They didn't make me rich, but they'll certainly give me a longer career." Why? Because she showed producers and directors that she not only had great range, but that she was willing to work in small-budget films as long as the part was right.

Next, Salma was off to Hungary to film the TNT movie, *The Hunchback of Notre Dame*. In the film, Salma played the female lead of Esmerelda, an enchanting, rebellious gypsy girl who wins the heart of the hunchback. Salma not only got the chance to travel but also to perform with honored actor Mandy Patinkin. On the set of the film, she also met the man who would become her longtime boyfriend, Edward Atterton. Edward, an English actor who would later be seen in *The Man in the Iron Mask*, also had a part in *Hunchback*, and he and Salma fell in love on the set. They were together for a few years, even living together in

Filmed on location in Hungary, *The Hunchback of Notre Dame* featured Salma as Esmerelda–an enchanting, rebellious gypsy girl. On the set, she also met the man who would become her longtime boyfriend, Edward Atterton.

Los Angeles, until they broke up in 1999.

Salma's luck spread from her personal life to her professional. Back in the States, a project was finally being put into action that had been close to Salma's heart for quite a while. The film was called *Fools Rush In.*

This movie was a big move for Salma in a lot of ways. First, it was a mainstream romantic comedy—something she'd never done before. Second, the lead female character was a strong Mexican woman—someone who wasn't just about being sexy. And lastly, Salma had a lot of input into the script.

When Salma first read the script for *Fools Rush In*, she was immediately attracted to it. "I liked that it took some really big chances. Most comedies are formulated—they keep it light, they don't want to get into any trouble," Salma said in an Eonline interview. "Those are the boring ones. This one doesn't quite fit into the formula. It risks some really heavy-duty, intense issues." Among those issues are pregnancy outside of marriage, interracial relationships, and making choices between career and family. But in the beginning, Salma didn't like some things about the script. And she didn't agree to play the role of Isabel Fuentes until those problems were addressed.

The story is about a Catholic Mexican American woman—Isabel—who meets a white Protestant man named Alex Whitman, played by *Friends'* Matthew Perry. The pair has a one-night stand, and Isabel gets pregnant. Then they fall in love and get married. But as the marriage progresses, certain issues come between the couple. Alex wants to move his new family back to New York, but Isabel wants to stay in Las Vegas to be near her family and her career. Isabel wants their baby to be Catholic, and Alex does not. Their parents clash, their cultures clash, and the pair almost breaks up because of all of this.

Salma originally objected to some stereotyping in the script. In an early version of the screenplay, Isabel was a tourist photographer at Caesar's Palace and nothing else. Salma wondered why she would object to moving with Alex and her baby to New York. The filmmakers told her it was because Isabel's family was in Nevada and family is important to Mexican women. Salma objected, saying Mexican women also love the men in their lives. Plus

Isabel was pregnant; her new family would be just as important to her as her parents were. If her support system and her love were in New York, Salma said, she'd go.

Salma suggested they give Isabel a career—something more solid to keep her rooted in Nevada. At her urging, they decided to make Isabel into an amazing photographer who had always had a dream to make a book about the desert. She's just raised enough money to put her dream into action, and so the last thing she wants to do is head off to New York. "That put her in touch with nature, made her sensitive and artistic, smart and ambitious," Salma told Eonline. "This also gives you a woman who is easier to fall in love with—not just this chiquita banana who snaps pictures in Caesar's Palace."

Fools Rush In was a mainstream hit, and Salma was suddenly thrust into the spotlight. But instead of running right out and starring in a bunch of big-budget blockbusters, Salma continued to perform in a mix of different films. Her next few career moves again displayed her willingness to break the mold and to keep the public guessing.

In 1998, Salma appeared in three very different movies. She played the part of Anita, a coat-check girl who dreams of being a famous singer, in the 1970s disco drama *54*. Salma had a lot of fun on the set, dressing in wild costumes and playing practical jokes on her costars, Breckin Meyer and Ryan Philippe. The movie was a critical disaster, but last-minute script changes and reshoots took the credit for that, while strong performances were given by everyone involved. Then, as a favor to her old friend, Salma played a small part in a teen horror flick called *The Faculty*, written by Kevin Williamson

Salma showed her talent for romantic comedy in the 1997 film *Fools Rush In*, co-starring with Matthew Perry from the hit TV series *Friends*.

and directed by Robert Rodriguez. From there, she went straight for a seriously independent, offbeat romantic comedy called *The Velocity of Gary*, which costarred Ethan Hawke.

None of these films got much attention from audiences or the press, but Salma's next string of films generated a huge amount of buzz—most of it not very good. In 1999's Kevin Smith film *Dogma*, Salma played Serendipity, a muse with writer's block. The film co-starred Matt

Damon, Ben Affleck, Chris Rock, Linda Fiorentino, and Alan Rickman and was basically about two fallen angels on a quest to get readmitted to heaven. Before the movie ever hit theaters, there was a lot of protest and controversy over what some people considered to be anti-Catholic themes. None of the hubbub bothered Salma, however. She was proud of her work and proud of the film.

"It's a small group of people that are always mad at everybody," Salma said of the protesters. "They created this organization to protest against things . . . I do understand that not everybody should like this film. And if they don't, then they shouldn't go see it." As always, Salma just stated her very straightforward opinion and washed her hands of the situation.

It wouldn't be so easy to ignore the critics on her next film, *Wild Wild West*. From the very beginning, Will Smith wanted Salma Hayek for the part of Rita Escobar in *Wild Wild West*— even though they'd only met once, backstage at the 1996 MTV Movie Awards. "I'm attracted to warm energy. The thing about comedy is, you have to relate to someone in order to find their comedy funny," Smith told *Premiere* magazine. "We feel closer to people who make us laugh. I had that with Salma." But the film's director, Barry Sonenfeld, wasn't so sure. He made Salma audition for six months and says he was never certain she was the right actress for the role. But once Salma was on set, she completely impressed him—so much that he increased her number of scenes from two to 18 and likened her to the comedic genius, Lucille Ball. Unfortunately, all these happy feelings and friendships couldn't help the film.

The history of the film *Wild Wild West* is the

classic tale of a big-budget flop. Starring mega-star Will Smith along with respected actors Kevin Kline, Kenneth Branagh, and Salma Hayek, the film had huge effects, huge sound, huge marketing . . . and almost no audience. It was mocked for its lack of plot and lack of humor, and many critics pegged it as the worst film of 1999. Still, a lot of people must have liked Salma's performance in the film, because she won the Blockbuster Award for Favorite Supporting Actress—an award voted upon by moviegoers. Ironically, in the same year, Salma's new production company, Venta-narosa, produced what was arguably one of the best films of the year, *El Coronel no tiene quien le escriba* (*No One Writes to the Colonel*).

The movie tells the story of a retired Mexican colonel and his wife who are struggling with poverty in the 1940s. Salma played the part of Julia, a woman who had a scandalous relation-ship with the couple's dead son. Even if it's not the most cheery plot ever written, the film won rave reviews. It was nominated for a foreign language Oscar, and won the Jury Prize in Latin American Cinema at the 2000 Sundance Film Festival.

Salma would wrap up this year of triumphs and failures with her most daring move yet—taking a part in the breakthrough film, *Time-code*. The movie was the first film ever shot entirely with a digital camera, but its innova-tions didn't stop there. The film told four stories simultaneously, each playing in one corner of the screen. Salma played a young woman trying to break into Hollywood—a role she could defi-nitely relate to. But while the part may not have been a stretch, the work was grueling. The film was entirely improvised and shot in one

continuous take. That means no script to fall back on and no breaks for coffee. Because of its technical breakthroughs, *Timecode* got a lot of press. Unfortunately it did not bring many people into theaters.

Salma's next movie, a comedy co-starring Steve Zahn called *Chain of Fools,* was never released in theaters. This was a disappointment to Salma, who thoroughly enjoyed making the film, but it was a disappointment she had to quickly put behind her. Not only was her movie about Frida Kahlo about to take off running, but a few other projects close to Salma's heart were ready to be put into production as well. Each of Salma's next few films had one very important thing in common—the one thing Salma had been struggling for since she first landed in Los Angeles—serious Latino content.

Here's Salma with co-star and recording artist Will Smith in a scene from their film *Wild Wild West.* Salma enjoyed the role and never let the film's lack of commercial success get her down.

NEVER FORGET YOUR ROOTS

Over the years, Salma has worked hard for a number of charities and causes. She is a spokesperson for the March of Dimes and appears in their ads to raise the public's awareness of this charity's work. Through her work as a model for Revlon, she also became involved with the Revlon Run/Walk for Breast Cancer Awareness, and she strives to educate Spanish-speaking communities about this disease. She has raised money for hunger-related charities, and she called some of her influential friends to urge them to donate money to flood relief in Chiapas in 1998. But of all the causes Salma has taken up, none is closer to her heart than that of gaining equality for Latino actors and actresses in Hollywood.

Salma takes exception when people mention the current success of Latino actors in Hollywood. "I think that if you look at the statistics, the hiring of Latino actors has dropped considerably," Salma said in a Mr. Showbiz interview. "Hey, I'm doing great, but I can't sit here and say, 'Yeah, *we're* doing great! Latino Power!' That's not true." In May of 1999 the Screen Actors Guild published a study that showed that Latinos are the most underrepresented ethnic group in entertainment. According to the findings,

As a model and spokesperson for Revlon cosmetics, Salma became involved with the Revlon Run/Walk for Breast Cancer Awareness.

Latino appearances in television and film is less than one-third of their proportion of the U.S. population.

Salma believes that statistics like this are disgraceful. Luckily, though, she thinks production companies are now slowly starting to get the picture. "They finally understand in this film industry which is entirely defined by money," Salma told *Vivamagazine,* "how many Latinos live in the United States. 32 million potential customers, a minority that is growing rapidly and above all it's enthusiastic about movies."

Even so, Salma has seen a lot of her friends, who have been auditioning in L.A. for as long as she has, go absolutely nowhere. Because she has managed to make a name for herself, Salma gets scripts that feature Latina women. But she says that when she turns the part down and mentions a list of women she knows who could do the job just as well, the movie doesn't get done because she's not in it. Producers want a star, but they're not willing to find someone new and turn her into a star.

Instead of sitting around hoping the situation will get better, Salma has gone out and gotten involved. Her production company, Ventanarosa, has made a deal with Sony to produce television programs in English for Columbia TriStar and in Spanish for Telemundo. Salma also likes to hold dinners and parties, inviting Latino artists to get together and make connections that might help them further their careers and gain exposure. "She's Central Station for Mexican filmmakers," Elizabeth Avellan told *Premiere.* The way Salma sees it, someone has to take the reigns and promote Latino projects. It's not going to happen on its own. More than anything, she's working for a time when Mexican and

In 1998 Salma used her high-profile status to urge donations for aid to Chiapas, Mexico after a devastating flood there.

Latino stereotypes will no longer be an issue.

"People in this town know Mexicans only as maids," Salma said to *George* magazine. "And they don't hesitate to tell you that when they're making a movie." She was even advised once to play down her Latino heritage in order to get parts. "I remember going to audition for a sci-fi film and the studio being aghast at the idea of a Mexican in space," Salma told *Scene*. "One casting director even told me I should take advantage of my middle-eastern sounding name and pretend I was Lebanese." But Salma is proud of her home country. She isn't about to deny where she came from.

She also isn't about to lose her accent. It's part

After winning much praise for her own work, Salma frequently appears at other awards presentations.

of her, and she wants Hollywood to accept her and appreciate her the way she is. The accent has become less pronounced over the years as she has become more skilled in English, but it shows no signs of disappearing. "I do work with a coach, but for me to get rid of it completely, I'd have to work with a coach 24 hours a day, every day, for months and months, and then work on the part for months," Salma told Mr. Showbiz. "I don't know that it's worth it. Why can't they just love me as I am?"

Still, she knows her accent does prevent her from getting some roles. When people compare her struggles in Hollywood with Jennifer Lopez's, Salma is quick to point out the difference. "She isn't Mexican. She grew up in New York," Salma says of Lopez. "She is a wonderful actress, but she doesn't have the same handicap as me because she can turn the Latin thing on as, and when, it is appropriate. It is more difficult for us actresses with the accent."

With so much opposition standing in her way, Salma decided it was time to take matters into her own hands. Aside from its television deal, Ventanarosa is now developing films that will depict important Latino stories of heroism and triumph. These films require extensive Latino casts and also feature the work of Latino screenwriters, directors, and crews. Salma is not going to stop until she shows the world not only that Latinos are great artists and filmmakers, but that they have a history rich with stories begging to be told.

"For Salma to come here and be a role model for Latinos is important," Nely Galan of Telemundo told *George* magazine. "It tells you a lot about the time we're in when a very Mexican woman has become a pop culture icon." And Salma is not just an icon; she's also a savvy actress and producer who works night and day to prove she's a force to be reckoned with.

"Salma will be an important producer," Barry Sonnenfeld, director of *Wild Wild West,* told *Premiere* magazine. "She is very ambitious, not in a sneaky way, but in wanting to produce and in caring about people and being sensitive but with a point of view."

One look at her upcoming projects shows that Salma's point of view is all about Latino power.

6

A BEAUTIFUL
FUTURE

"I 've come to the point where, if Hollywood doesn't give me the parts I want, I'm at the place where I can supply them myself," Salma told *Premiere*. "Because I do believe in myself even if they don't." Salma has proved she is more than willing to go out there and make it happen for herself. This is evident in her upcoming work—four diverse films, all with Latino-heavy casts, which will all gain wide release in the United States in 2001.

First up is the star-packed movie *Traffic*. This film, starring Michael Douglas, Dennis Quaid, Don Cheadle, and Catherine Zeta-Jones is about drug trafficking between Latin America and the United States. The story is a complicated one, showing all sides of the drug-trafficking process and the people who fight against it. From the United States drug czar and his family, to the family of the Latino drug lord who is arrested and ripped away from his wife and home, the film tells the personal stories of the various people involved. Salma took a small part in this groundbreaking film—a dramatic, harsh look into an ongoing international struggle.

Traffic opened in late December 2000 in New York and Los

After becoming the single most recognizable actress in all of Mexico, Salma now has a worldwide following. Here she waves to adoring fans at the Cannes Film Festival in France.

Angeles in order to be eligible for Oscar consideration. About a month before these premieres, Salma wrapped production on a film she both produced and starred in called *En el tiempo de las mariposas (In the Time of Butterflies)*. The film is based on the Julia Alvarez novel of the same name and is about three sisters from the Dominican Republic who found the strength to stand up to an evil dictator.

Alvarez's novel was a fictionalization of the true story of the Mirabal sisters, Minerva, Maria Teresa, Patria, and Dede. According to the novel, the eldest sister, Minerva, slapped dictator Rafael Leonidas Trujillo when he made advances toward her at a dance. Later, Trujillo had her father arrested in revenge. This sparked three of the sisters (Dede excluded) to start a resistance movement against the dictator. Their rebellious, heroic lives ended when they were murdered by secret police. Dede, who had chosen to remove herself from the conflict, was the family's only survivor.

Salma was moved by the story, and signed on not only to star as the strong character of Minerva but to co-produce the film. The film was directed by Spaniard Mariano Barroso and co-stars singer Marc Anthony and revered Latino actor Edward James Olmos as Trujillo. The movie, which was filmed in Mexico City, Morelos, and Veracruz, allowed Salma to return home for a while in 2000, as some scenes were shot in her hometown of Coatzacoalcos. When she was granted the rare gift of free time, she thoroughly enjoyed it by visiting with family and friends. The film wrapped production on November 25, 2000, which was, ironically, the 40th anniversary of the real Mirabel sisters' deaths. The movie airs on Showtime in 2001.

In 2001, viewers in the States also have the opportunity to see another of Salma's projects that has already enjoyed success overseas. Released in Spain and Italy in the spring of 2000, *La Gran Vida* (*Living it Up*) is a wacky romantic comedy that was filmed entirely in Spain. It was Salma's first movie to be made in that country. According to *Variety*, Salma was cast as the film's female lead in order to gain a U.S. audience—evidence of the fact that people around the world respect her star power.

The film is about a young man named Martin who decides to take his own life. He goes through some failed attempts, and when he's about to jump from a bridge, he's visited by a "fairy godfather." This godfather tells Martin he'll give him a million dollars if he waits to kill himself. The problem is, he has to spend the money in two weeks' time, since that's when this million dollars is due back to the gangsters the godfather

In her recent film, *Traffic*, Salma co-starred with Michael Douglas, Catherine Zeta-Jones, and Benicio Del Toro in a complex story that examines all sides of the international drug trade.

"borrowed" it from; if the money's not paid back in time, the gangsters will likely kill Martin. This way, Martin gets what he wants—his own death—but he gets to have some fun first.

Martin throws himself a huge party with the money, inviting a ton of perfect strangers because he has no friends. At the bash he meets Lola, a beautiful waitress played by Salma Hayek, and instantly falls in love with her. At first, she wants nothing to do with him, but he doesn't give up. When it starts to look like Martin might have a chance with Lola, he decides he doesn't want to die after all. Now he has to find a way to pay back the million dollars so that he can live and be with Lola.

The film earned mixed reviews in Spain but did solid box-office business. The plot may sound a bit complex, but Columbia TriStar thought it was funny and accessible enough that the company is currently in negotiations to buy the U.S. rights to the film. Casting Salma in the lead role to get U.S. interest was the right move.

Last, but certainly not least, is Salma's baby— the biographical film of Frida Kahlo which finally went into production in January of 2001, a subject Salma told *Scene* she could "talk about all day." Unfortunately, before the project ever got off the ground, there was a snag that the press couldn't seem to stop talking about.

While Miramax was still struggling to find just the right director for the film, a crushing announcement was made: Jennifer Lopez was also developing a film about the life of Frida Kahlo and was rushing to get her film into production before Salma's. With legendary film director Francis Ford Coppola signed on as producer, and *La Bamba* director Luis Valdez set to helm the film, Lopez seemed to have one up on

Salma. Both films were slated to go into production in the winter of 2000/2001.

The press has always liked to pit Lopez against Salma, printing stories about how the two leading Latina actresses dislike each other. (Whether or not this is true is unclear.) When news broke that both women wanted to make almost the same film, the Hollywood press ate it up, running dozens of stories updating the world on the progress of both films. Salma was quoted as saying, "This movie should be played by a Mexican. . . . I want to tell this story about my country and my people." Lopez, a New York-born actress of Puerto Rican descent, told reporters,

Salma looks forward to expanding her range in a variety of films—films that challenge her, films that make her laugh, films with a message.

"I do not know Salma Hayek. We do not have a personal relationship. Hollywood has been full of projects on Kahlo for 10 years. It is not an exclusive right of Salma, although Frida was Mexican like her."

But Salma did not want to get into a catfight about something that meant so much to her. She simply went about preparing for her role and executing her producing duties on her film. She seems to have decided to do the best work possible, and let the public decide which Frida Kahlo film is worth seeing. If she has her way, we will see hers before the end of 2001.

Looking toward the future, Salma simply wants to continue to work in a variety of films—

Even after becoming a well-established and successful Hollywood actress, Salma is still forced to fight against being stereotyped as a "fiery Latina." What's Salma's response to this type of prejudice? "Whenever they put me in this category, I just try to make the roll more interesting."

films that challenge her, films that make her laugh, films with a message. She's said that the actors she'd most like to work with are Sean Penn, Daniel Day-Lewis, and Johnny Depp, because she prefers interesting men over handsome men. She also loves to play all kinds of women, and would like to work in more comedies, although she does admit "they never seem to give the comic parts to the pretty girls." Always the realist, Salma knows she may continue to be stereotyped, but now she knows how to handle it. "When they look for somebody with fire, Salma Hayek comes to their mind," Salma told *Vivamagazine*. "Whenever they put me in this category, I just try to make the roles more interesting. And since I now have a place at the negotiating table, I can try to get other roles for myself."

She will continue to fight stereotyping though, and hopes for the day when Latino actors will be considered for all roles on an equal plane with all other ethnicities. "[People say], 'OK, we wrote a part for a Latino. Bring in a Latino.' But people say. 'OK, we have a man here who's lost a child, who's lost a job, and goes into a middle age crisis and is trying to rebuild his life.' They should open the door for Latino actors to come and audition for that," Salma said in Mr. Showbiz interview. "Even if it doesn't say it's a

Latino guy. It's just a conflict that anyone can go through, that he can go through."

When it comes to other aspects of the movie business, many actors see directing as a natural step in their careers. But Salma knows directing is a an entirely different part of the art form—one she's not yet willing to tackle. When a reporter asked her if directing was the logical next move for her, Salma responded, "Why logical? I am not that presumptuous to believe I can do everything now. Directing is again a whole different ball game. I just have too much respect for that."

In the meantime, Salma will continue to balance her acting and producing duties with her charitable work and her social life. She enjoys attending the swank parties and events to which she is invited. And she makes the most of her occasional appearances on award shows like the first ever VH1 My Music Awards, where she introduced the Red Hot Chili Peppers by calling them her favorite band. When Salma isn't with her boyfriend, Edward Norton Jr., she likes to do low-key things with her close friends.

"I don't do the Hollywood thing," Salma told *Scene.* "Although I see Renee Zellweger and Ashley Judd when they're in town. George Clooney is a friend. I prefer cooking dinner and playing Taboo." And then there are those private parties she hosts to bring together Latino filmmakers. All in all, Salma keeps herself very busy in all aspects of her life. And she wants to keep it that way.

"I hope there'll be lots and lots more movies ahead of me," Salma told *Vivamagazine.* "And if I'm very lucky, maybe there'll be one amongst them that's going to be a classic one day."

If Salma continues to work as hard as she does now, she's sure to make that happen.

CHRONOLOGY

1968   Salma Hayek Jiminez is born on September 2 in Coatzacoalcos, Veracruz, Mexico.

1981   Salma moves to Louisiana to attend Catholic school.

1983   Salma is expelled and moves back to Mexico.

1984   Graduates from high school, later begins her studies at Universidad Iberoamericana.

1986   Leaves school for a career in acting.

1989   Salma is discovered by a soap opera producer and lands a role on *Un Nuevo amanecer;* lands the lead role in *Teresa;* wins two TV Novela Awards—one for Best Newcomer and one for Best Actress.

1991   Leaves Mexico and moves to Hollywood where she studies acting with Stella Adler.

1993   Wins a role in *Mi vida loca* and earns her SAG card.

1995   *Desperado* premieres; Salma is nominated for a Silver Ariel Award for *El Callejon de los milagros* which premiered this year.

1996   *From Dusk Til Dawn* premieres; Salma meets longtime love Edward Atterton on the set of *The Hunchback of Notre Dame;* Salma is chosen as one of *People*'s 50 Most Beautiful People; Salma is nominated for Best Kiss, along with Antonio Banderas at the MTV Movie Awards.

1997   *Fools Rush In* premieres; Salma becomes a spokesperson for Revlon.

1998   *54* premieres; Salma wins the Nosostros Golden Eagle Award for Best Actress in Film.

1999   Salma ends her relationship with Edward Atterton; she begins dating Ed Norton Jr.; *Dogma* premieres; *El Colonel no tiene quien le escriba* premieres; *Wild Wild West* premieres; Salma is nominated for an ALMA award.

2000   *Timecode* premieres; *El Colonel no tiene quien le escriba*
          wins the Jury Prize in Latin American Cinema at the
          Sundance Film Festival; Salma wins a Blockbuster
          Entertainment Award for *Wild Wild West.*

2001   *In the Time of Butterflies* premieres on Showtime; Frida
          Kahlo premieres.

ACCOMPLISHMENTS

Filmography

1988	*Un Nuevo Amanecer* (TV Series)
1989	*Teresa* (TV Series)
1993	*Mi vida loca* (*My Crazy Life*)
1995	*El Callejon de los milagros* (*Miracle Alley*) *Desperado* *Four Rooms* *Fair Game*
1996	*From Dusk Til Dawn* *Fled*
1997	*Fools Rush In* *The Hunchback of Notre Dame* (TV Movie) *Breaking Up*
1998	*54* *The Faculty* *The Velocity of Gary*
1999	*Dogma* *El Colonel no tiene quien le escriba* (*No One Writes to the Colonel*) *Wild Wild West*
2000	*Timecode* *Chain of Fools* *Traffic* *La Gran vida* (*Living it Up*)
2001	*En el tiempo de las mariposas* (*In the Time of Butterflies*) *Frida Kahlo*

Awards

1989	TV Novela Best Newcomer Award for *Nuevo Amanecer* TV Novela Best Actress Award for *Teresa*
1995	Nominated for a Best Actress Silver Ariel Award for *Miracle Alley*

1996	Nominated with Antonio Banderas for Best Kiss at the MTV Movie Awards for *Desperado*
1998	Nosostros Golden Eagle Award for Best Actress in Film
1999	Nominated for an American Latino Media Arts Award for Outstanding Actress in a Feature Film for *54*
1999	Diversity Award for Outstanding Diversity Success Story
1999	Nominated for an American Latino Media Arts Award for Outstanding Actress in a Feature Film for *Wild Wild West*
2000	Blockbuster Entertainment Favorite Supporting Actress Award for *Wild Wild West*

FURTHER READING

Duncan, Patricia J. Salma Hayek. New York, St. Martin's, 1999.

Morris, Bob. "Mexican Firecracker." *George,* July 1999.

McDonough, Kevin. "Salma Hayek: Changing the Rules." *Biography,* September 2000.

Friedman, Vanessa. "Dressing Up." *Elle,* April 2000.

Hemblade, Christopher. "Sole Diva." *Scene,* August 1999.

Hofler, Robert. "The Wild One." *Premiere,* June 1999.

INDEX

PHOTO CREDITS:

2: The Everett Collection
6: Gregg DeGuire/ London Features International
9: Bettmann/Corbis
12: Munawar Hasain/ Foto International/ Archive Photos
14: Charles & Josette Lenars/Corbis
17: Gregg DeGuire/London Features International
20: Fitzroy Barrett/ Globe Photos
22: Alan Mothner/ AP/Wide World Photos
27: Cris Weeks/Liaison Agency/Corbis
31: Photofest
32: Gregg DeGuire/ London Features International
37: Photofest
40: Photofest
43: Photofest
44: Dennis Van Tine/ London Features International
47: Reuters/Fred Prouser/ Archive Photos
48: Dennis Van Tine/ London Features International
50: Fitzroy Barrett/ Globe Photos
53: Reuters NewMedia Inc./Corbis
55: Roger Harvey/ Globe Photos
56: Gregg DeGuire/ London Features International

Cover photo: ©Dennis Van Tine/London Features

ABOUT THE AUTHOR

KIERAN SCOTT graduated with honors from Rutgers University in New Brunswick, New Jersey, with a B.A. in English and journalism. She is the author of numerous young adult and middle-grade fiction and non-fiction books, including biographies on Cameron Diaz, Leonardo DiCaprio, Matt Damon, and James Van Der Beek. Formerly the editor of popular young adult series, Kieran is now a full-time writer. Her favorite Salma Hayek movie is *Fools Rush In.*